A Kid's Guide to Drawing™

How to Draw
Cars
Laura Murawski

The Rosen Publishing Group's
PowerKids Press™
New York

Published in 2001 by The Rosen Publishing Group, Inc.
29 East 21st Street, New York, NY 10010

First Edition

Book Design: Kim Sonsky

Illustration Credits: Laura Murawski

Photo Credits: Title page (hand) by Arlan Dean; p. 6 © Corbis; p. 8 © SuperStock; p. 10 © SuperStock; p. 12 © David Reed/Corbis; p. 14 © Jack Sullivan Photography; p. 16 © Neil Rabinowitz/Corbis; p. 18 © Corbis; p. 20 © Ron Kimball.

Murawski, Laura.
    How to draw cars / Laura Murawski.—1st ed.
        p. cm.— (A kid's guide to drawing)
    Includes index.
    Summary: Describes how to draw various cars, including the Benz three-wheeler, Volkswagen Beetle, and McLaren F1.
    ISBN 0-8239-5548-6 (alk. paper)
    1. Automobiles in art—Juvenile literature. 2. Drawing—Technique—Juvenile literature. [1. Automobiles in art. 2. Drawing—Technique.] I. Title.

NC825.A8 M87 2000
743'.89629222—dc21   00-028040

Manufactured in the United States of America

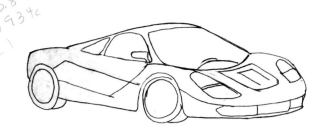

CONTENTS

Let's Get Rolling

Learning how to draw cars is fun and easy! Have you ever sat in a car and wondered how it works? Have you ever wanted to drive a car yourself? Well, you are not old enough to drive yet, but you are old enough to think about your dream car. There are many different kinds of cars. Cars have basic parts, such as tires, engines, **bumpers**, and **fenders**. Each car has a special look that tells us something about when it was made. In this book, you will learn about eight cars, from an 1885 three-wheeler to a 1999 hot rod! You'll learn how to draw them, too.

Here's what you'll need to draw cars:
- A sketch pad
- A number 2 pencil / Pen
- A pencil sharpener
- An eraser

In this book you will learn how to draw most of the cars in eight steps. Most of the drawings begin with <u>rectangles</u> or <u>circles</u>. There are directions under each drawing to help you through each step. Each new step is shown in color to help guide you.

Drawing cars is a lot easier than you might think. The basic shapes you use to draw cars are rectangles, circles, and <u>triangles</u>. These shapes and other drawing shapes and terms are explained in the Drawing Terms list on page 22 of this book. Be sure to check out the Drawing Terms section if you run into words or shapes you don't understand in the step-by-step directions. It will help you out!

To draw cars, follow the four Ps: **Patience**, **Persistence**, Practice, and a Positive **attitude**. The more you draw, the better you will become at it. Before you start, make sure you find a quiet, clean, and well-lit space where you will be able to pay attention to your drawings. Good luck, and most important, have fun! Now sharpen your pencils, and let's get rolling!

The Benz Three-Wheeler

In 1885, Karl Benz made the first motor car. Karl Benz was a German **engineer**. Unlike the cars of today, his car had only three wheels. There were two wheels in the back, and one wheel in the front. The car had a two-stroke engine. The two-stroke engine let the test **model** of this car go at a speed of only eight miles (12.9 km) per hour. Some cars today can go as fast as 276 miles (444 km) per hour or faster! Although the Benz Three-Wheeler was built more than 100 years ago, it used some parts that are still used in today's cars.

1

Draw three <u>circles</u>. Notice how the circle farthest to the left is larger than the one that crosses it. The circle that is farthest to the right is the smallest, and placed a little below the other two circles.

2

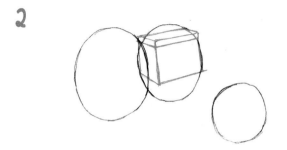

Next, draw a <u>three-dimensional (3-D) box</u> inside the middle circle. The box should look like it has a lid on top.

3

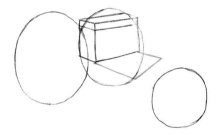

Draw two lines from the bottom left and right corners of your 3-D box. Connect the lines to make a funny-shaped <u>rectangle</u>.

4

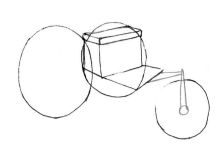

Draw two lines that come to a point (from the funny-shaped rectangle). Now draw two more lines that start from the point made by the first lines. These lines should begin in a point and then widen a little. Draw a tiny circle at the end of the second set of lines.

5

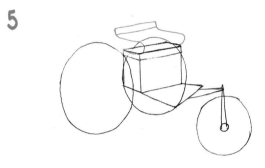

Draw two <u>curved lines</u> on top of the 3-D box. Join them by adding a small rectangle at the top of the curved lines.

6

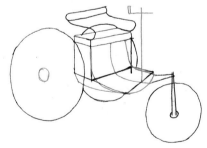

Finish the drawing by curving the lines of the funny-shaped rectangle and the front sides of the box. Add a small circle inside the biggest circle. Then add a <u>vertical line</u> and draw a handle (which looks like the letter "L" lying down) at the top of this line.

The Ford Model T

Henry Ford made the Model T in 1908 in Detroit, Michigan. With the Model T car, Henry Ford changed the way cars were built. He was the first person to use an assembly line to build cars. In an assembly line, each worker adds one piece or does one small job that helps make the car. Each person does their special job for each car made. This makes it easier and cheaper to build cars. The Ford Model T was built this way, so it was inexpensive. Many people could afford to buy the Model T, not just rich people. The cost of the car was not the only thing that made the Ford Model T so popular. It was also easy to drive and did not need a lot of care. The Model T **outsold** all other types of cars for almost 19 years.

1

Begin by drawing a <u>3-D rectangle</u>. This shape willl be the guide line for your drawing.

2

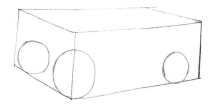

Now draw three circles (for wheels) inside the rectangle. Notice the three sizes and where the circles are placed.

3

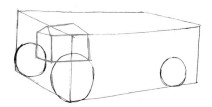

Next, draw a shape like a house at the front end of the rectangle. You just drew the grille, or front end, and the engine of the Ford Model T!

4

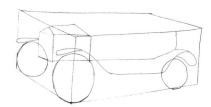

Draw curved lines above the circles to make the fenders. Add a vertical line to the back of the car.

5

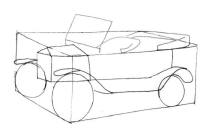

Now draw the front window by drawing a <u>slanted</u> rectangle. Draw curved lines to make the front and back seats.

6

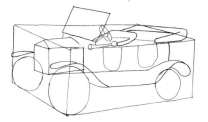

Now draw in the details of the car. Draw the steering wheel and the car horn. Draw in the two car doors by making two <u>"U" shapes</u>.

7

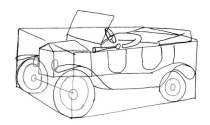

Draw small circles (for headlights) on the house shape. Draw two smaller circles inside each wheel. Connect the small circles on the front wheels with a <u>horizontal line</u>.

8

Draw small vertical lines on the grille and seats. Erase any extra lines.

The Bugatti 41 Royale, Coupe de Ville

Ettore Bugatti was the designer of the Bugatti 41 Royale. Ettore had many talents. As a teenager, he studied art. Ettore decided not to become an artist, though. He became more interested in motor cars. In 1898, he gave up art and built his first car. Ettore began his own car company in 1910. He soon became known for making and racing fast cars. Although the Bugatti race, or sports, cars were very successful, Ettore wanted to make a **luxury** car. He was known for making fast cars, not luxury cars. Ettore decided to try to build the most **elegant** car he could. He named this car the Bugatti Royale. This model was built from 1929 to 1932. During that time, though, only eight Bugatti Royales were made because they were so expensive.

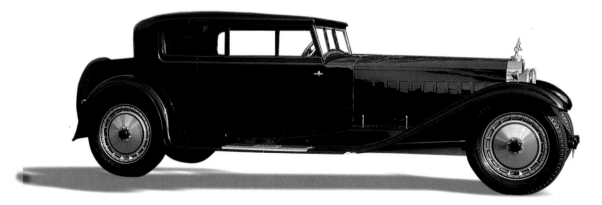

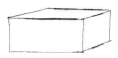

Draw a 3-D box.

To the left of this box, draw a taller 3-D box. The second box should touch the first one.

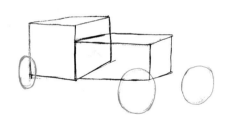

Draw three circles to make the wheels. Notice that the circles are different sizes. Notice where they are placed and whether or not they cross the 3-D boxes.

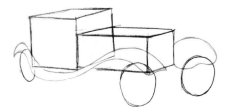

Next, draw curved lines as shown to make the car's fenders.

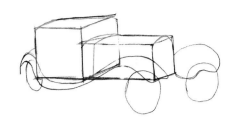

Now round the top corners of the 3-D boxes. Add curved lines as shown for detail.

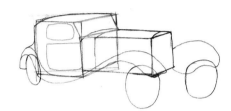

Add a <u>tilted</u> rectangle (for a front window) to the top of the taller 3-D box. Add an <u>oval</u> (window) and <u>square</u> (door) on the side.

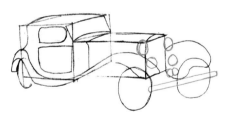

Draw five small circles at the front of the shorter 3-D box. This is the front of the car. The small circles are the car's headlights and horns.

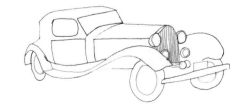

Draw smaller circles inside the three big circles. Draw vertical lines in the grille. Erase any extra lines.

The Volkswagen Beetle

The Volkswagen Beetle came from Germany. The German word *Volkswagen* means "people's car." Ferdinand Porsche, an Austrian engineer and car designer, and Adolf Hitler, Germany's leader from 1933 to 1945, came up with the idea for this inexpensive car. Soon after World War II (1939–45) the Volkswagen Beetle was brought to the United States. It was not popular at first because of its link with Hitler. He was known for his **cruelty** throughout World War II. Only two Beetles were sold in the United States in 1949! The Beetle's great price, design, and handling, though, eventually made it a big success. In 1968, there were 423,008 Volkswagen Beetles sold in the United States!

1

Draw a 3-D box. The box should look like it has a lid on top.

2

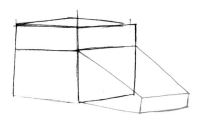

Now draw lines out from the 3-D box to form the <u>3-D triangle</u> shown.

3

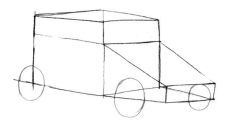

Next, draw three circles for the wheels. Notice that the circle farthest to the right is smaller than the first two circles.

4

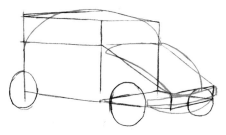

Now round the top corners of the 3-D box. Next, curve the lines on the top, front, and sides of the triangular shape.

5

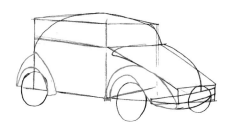

Draw curved lines above the two largest wheels. These are the fenders of the Beetle.

6

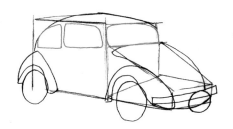

Draw three rectangles with rounded edges in the front and side of the 3-D box's lid. These shapes are the car's windows.

7

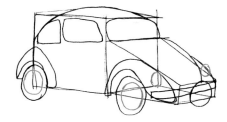

Add two small circles to the front of the car for headlights. Then draw two smaller circles inside the larger circles that form the wheels.

8

Add a square for the side door and erase extra lines to finish your car.

The Chevrolet Bel Air Sport Coupe

From 1953 to 1957, a car **manufacturer** called Chevrolet was making many different types of sports cars. In 1955, Chevrolet made the Bel Air Sport Coupe, which soon became famous. The Bel Air was special because of its V-8 engine, which made the car go very fast. The V-8 engine had a few nicknames. It was called the "Turbo-Fire," "the Red-Hot Hill Flattener," and the "Hot One." The Bel Air was driven as a race car in many car races. In 1955, a Bel Air won a big National Association for Stock Car Automobile Racing (NASCAR) race. The Bel Air did so well as a racing car that it was chosen to be the **Official Pace Car** for the Indianapolis 500 car race in 1955.

1

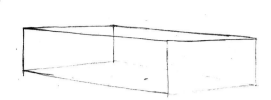

Draw a long 3-D rectangle.

2

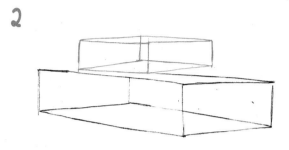

Next, draw a smaller 3-D rectangle just above the long 3-D rectangle.

3

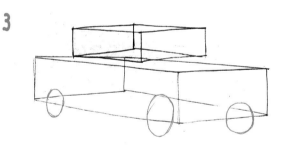

Draw three circles to make the wheels. Notice their different sizes and where they are placed on the 3-D rectangle.

4

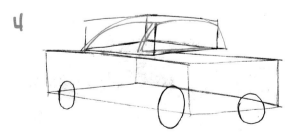

Next, draw the roof by rounding off the top and sides of the rectangle.

5

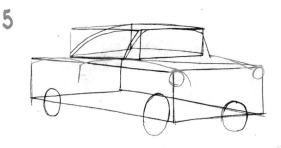

Now add curved lines to the top of the long 3-D rectangle to shape the body of the car. Add two small circles at the front for headlights.

6

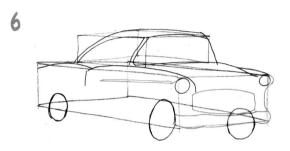

Next, draw a line on the side of the long 3-D rectangle as shown. Draw a curved rectangle on the front of the car.

7

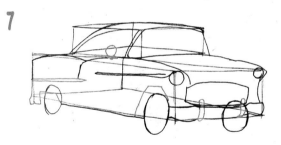

Draw a rearview mirror by making a small circle on top of the long 3-D rectangle. Draw in the bumper as shown on the front.

8

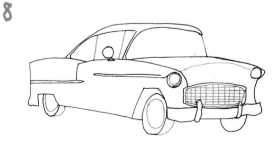

Add two vertical lines to make a side window. Add lines to the grille. Erase any extra lines.

The Shelby AC Cobra

The Shelby AC Cobra is one of the most amazing sports cars ever built. Carroll Shelby made the Shelby AC Cobra in 1961. Carroll had served as a **military** pilot in World War II (1939–45). He also liked to race cars. By racing, Carroll learned a lot about cars. In 1960, Carroll had to stop racing cars because he got hurt. This did not end Carroll's work with race cars, though. He dreamed of building a fast sports car. Carroll had an idea. He wanted to combine the **features** from a British sports car, called the AC Bristol, with the poweful V-8 engine of the American Ford. The result was the Shelby AC Cobra. The Shelby AC Cobra was the fastest sports car on the road in 1961.

1

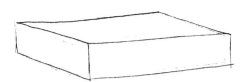

Start by drawing a long, flat 3-D rectangle.

2

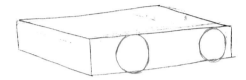

Now draw two circles on one side of the rectangle to make the wheels.

3

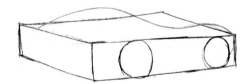

Draw a long <u>wavy line</u> across the rectangle to make the body of the Shelby.

4

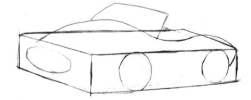

Next, draw three sides of a rectangle on top of the wavy line to form the windshield. Draw an oval to make the car's grille.

5

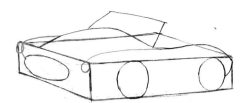

Draw two small circles near the oval for headlights. Draw curved lines out from the headlights toward the back of the car.

6

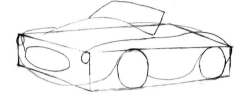

Add curved lines (as shown) to give more detail to the shape of the car.

7

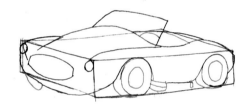

Draw circles inside the wheels to make the tires. Draw in curved shapes for the steering wheel and exhaust pipe.

8

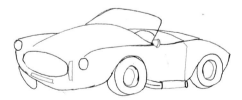

Add the rearview mirror next to the steering wheel. Add curved line in the wheels to make them look deeper. Add a small rectangle below the grille. Erase any extra lines.

The McLaren F1

The McLaren F1 is one of the fastest cars in the world today. Its average recorded speed is about 237 miles (381 km) per hour! That's double the speed of most cars. The McLaren is expensive, too. The cost of the McLaren is $1,131,120.00. Yes, that's right. It costs over one million dollars! That's probably why only 100 McLarens have been sold. The McLaren is not popular as a car for everyday driving because many features have been taken out so the car can go fast. The McLaren is a great race car, though. A McLaren F1 won first place in 1995 at the famous Le Mans 24-hour car race.

1

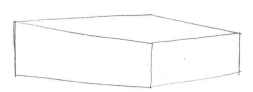

Begin by drawing a 3-D rectangle. Make the back slightly higher than the front.

2

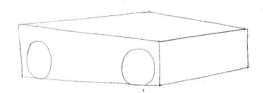

Now draw two circles for the tires.

3

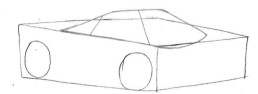

Draw the roof by making the shape shown on top of the rectangle. Draw two lines in this shape to begin forming the windows.

4

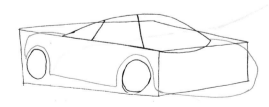

Draw the body of the McLaren by making a curved line circling around the car.

5

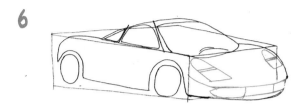

Draw in the windows by making the shapes shown. Draw two curved lines to make the steering wheel and dash board.

6

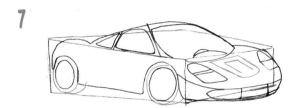

Now draw the headlights as shown. Draw in the bumper using curved horizontal lines.

7

Draw in the design on the hood of the McLaren. To make the tires, add circles around the circles you drew for wheels.

8

Add the rearview mirror. Draw the design lines on the side of the car. Erase any extra lines.

19

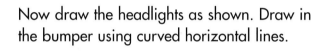

The Plymouth Prowler

The Chrysler Motor Company introduced the first Plymouth car in 1928. The idea to name a type of car the Plymouth came from American history. Plymouth was a **colony** in Massachusetts that was set up by the Puritans. The Puritans came to America on the *Mayflower* in 1620. The name Plymouth was meant to be a reminder of the good qualities of the Puritans. Two of these qualities were strength and achievement. The Plymouth Prowler was first shown at the North American International Auto Show in Detroit in 1993. It was not yet for sale, but it was a big hit! People liked that the whole body of the car was made of **aluminum**. The Prowler was already a popular car when it went on sale in 1997.

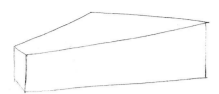

Start by drawing a shape like a 3-D triangle.

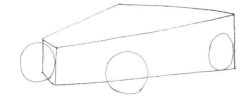

Next, draw three circles (for wheels) within the triangular shape. Notice the circles' shapes and sizes and where they are placed.

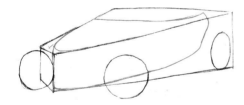

Now draw a curved shape as shown inside the triangular shape to make the body of the Prowler.

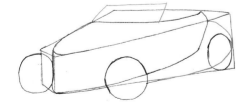

Draw a slanted shape for the windshield. Draw a curved line from the back of the curved shape (body) to the (right) front tire.

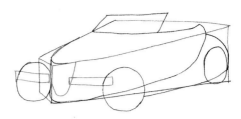

Next, draw two rectangles in front to make the bumper. Draw a "U" shape for the grille.

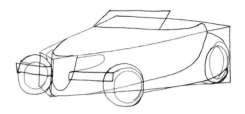

Now draw smaller circles inside the wheels to make tires. Draw fenders on top of the front wheels. Draw a curved line out from grille.

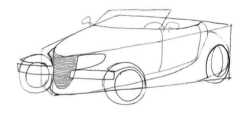

Draw a curved line for the steering wheel. Draw rearview mirrors on both sides. Draw lines to shape the door. Add small horizontal lines for detail on the grille.

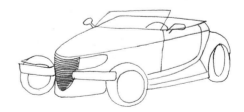

You're done! Erase any extra lines. You did a great job!

Drawing Terms

Here are some of the words and shapes you will need to draw cars.

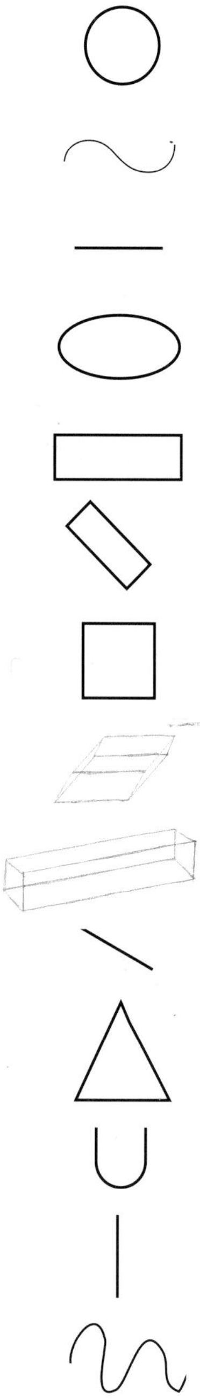

○ circle

∿ curved lines

— horizontal line

⬭ oval

▭ rectangle

◇ slanted (rectangle)

☐ square

▱ 3-D (three-dimensional) box

▱ 3-D (three-dimensional) rectangle

＼ tilted

△ triangle

∪ "U" shapes

| vertical line

〰 wavy line

Glossary

aluminum (uh-LOO-muh-num) A type of metal.

attitude (AH-tih-tood) A person's outlook or position toward a fact or situation.

bumpers (BUM-perz) A usually metal bar at the front and back of a car that prevents damage if the car is hit.

colony (KAH-luh-nee) An area in a new country where a large group of people move, who are still ruled by the leaders and laws of their old country.

cruelty (KROOL-tee) Actions that are mean and hurtful.

elegant (EH-lih-gint) Showing good taste.

engineer (en-jih-NEER) A person who is an expert at planning and building engines, machines, roads, bridges, and canals.

features (FEE-churz) The special look or form of a person or object.

fenders (FEHN-derz) Guards, usually metal, that go over the wheels of a car.

luxury (LUK-sher-ee) Something that is nice or expensive but is not really needed.

manufacturer (man-yoo-FAK-cher-er) A person or company that makes something by hand or with a machine.

military (MIH-lih-ter-ee) The part of a country's government that protects the country.

model (MOH-dil) An early draft version of something that will later be made.

Offical Pace Car (uh-FIH-shul PAYS CAHR) A car used in racing to let the other cars know where they are supposed to be.

outsold (owt-SOLD) Sold more than something else.

patience (PAY-shunts) The ability to wait calmly for something.

persistence (per-SIS-tehns) The ability to continue to do something without giving up.

Index

Web Sites

To learn more about drawing cars, check out this Web site:

http://www.epcomm.com/draw50/draw50.htm